The story of

What a place Skegness would have beer

Think tropical island. Long, unpeopled s........ .. sandy beach, the tide gently lapping against the sands, warm sunshine, a soft breeze.

Or perhaps not.

For a more realistic snapshot, make a trip 11 miles up the coast to Huttoft Car Terrace, then take the few steps over the sea-bank. What do you see?

The scene is desolate. A windswept and barren expanse, discarded rubbish from maritime traffic dotted on the sand, a grey and unwelcoming sea.

Even when the sun shines, the setting is inhospitable.

More likely, this would have been the Skegness of the mid-18th Century, home to a tiny community – just a few families eking out a living by fishing from rudimentary boats and scouring the beach for anything of possible sustenance, lost or dumped from cargo vessels plying their trade from East Coast ports to the Continent.

Fast forward to the present.

In an Andrew Lloyd-Webber stage musical, Michael Ball crooned "Love changes everything".

So does time.

Skegness – once such a barren and unwelcoming spot – is now one of Britain's Four Famous Seaside Sisters.

Along with Blackpool, Brighton and Scarborough, it has become a Premier League coastal resort.

To maintain the football terminology, while other seaside towns have had to take an early bath, Skegness is challenging for a place in Europe.

The status is not just a phenomenon of the post 1939-45 war era – or of the 1950s and 1960s when Prime Minister Harold Macmillan famously declared: "You've never had it so good."

James Wright, Friskney
(ISBN 1-902871-00-6)

Dating way back to the 1880s, perhaps a little before, the town has been a magnet for generations of visitors from the great industrial towns and cities of the East Midlands and Yorkshire – Derby, Leicester, Nottingham, Sheffield and beyond.

Spending a day, a week or even the whole of spring, summer and autumn in Skegness is not something these city folk deliberate about in advance.

It is something they just do – as if by instinct.

It is an activity embedded in their family consciousness and tradition – like trimming up a festive tree in the front room before Christmas or buying chocolate eggs at Easter.

Call it "swarm logic" or whatever you like, it reflects a loyalty that has been of immense and longstanding benefit to Skegness.

It constantly regenerates and revitalises the resort. Long may it continue!

Who created Skegness? In about the year 50 AD, the Romans came and saw.

Then, probably near the beginning of the fifth century, they went away again, leaving evidence of their saltmaking industry but not much else.

What about Roman Bank? Did they not construct this four-mile stretch of road and sea defence between Skegness and Ingoldmells?

Apparently not. By the time this was created, the centurions had long gone. The name is a fiction coined many centuries later.

Before the Roman invasion, this part of Lincolnshire was occupied by the Coritani tribe.

Then after the Romans left, the Saxons arrived.

In the ninth century, it was the turn of the Norse who arrived in their longboats as part of a massive invasion of eastern England.

In the process, Skegness assumed an identity. The invaders gave it a lasting name.

'Skeg' is the Old Norse for beard, while 'ness' means headland. The coastline off Lincolnshire is constantly changing and, 1,150 years ago, there probably was a headland – perhaps shaped like a beard.

What of the suggestion that there was a ruler named Skeg or Skeggi? Where is the evidence of such a man? It remains a theory, but unproven.

The Norse are invariably characterised as plunderers, ravagers, brutes – periodically sweeping in from the sea to kill, rape, pillage and destroy.

2

It was a reputation established with the raid on the monastery at Lindisfarne in 793 – an early lesson on how to obtain luxury goods, such as gold, silver and bejewelled books, with minimum resistance.

Further south, this specific location on the East Coast perhaps had no monasteries to be sacked and pillaged.

But at least its flat beaches provided easy landing for the famous longboats.

The sea was full of fish, and the even, fertile land could scarcely be surpassed for farming livestock – cattle, goats, pigs and sheep – and for growing vegetables and grain (including barley for beer).

The Norse were not merely marauding thugs. They were intrepid explorers, master shipbuilders and farmers.

They were also skilled craftsfolk, fashioning exquisite brooches from gold, silver and bronze, and carving stone tablets with floral motifs or runic inscriptions.

More is the regret, therefore, that their presence in Skegness has been so little researched – or at least so little recorded.

Whatever contribution the Norse settlers may have made, almost another 900 years were to pass before inspiration first flickered for what Skegness was to become.

It came not here but some 200 miles away on the South Coast where, in the 1750s, a Brighton doctor named Richard Russell suggested that the salt in seawater may have therapeutic properties.

Hitherto, brine had been used to treat people bitten by mad dogs, but as a medication for few if any other ailments.

The prescription from Russell to his patients was one of total bodily immersion followed by consumption of a tumbler of the sea itself. Ugh!

But Russell's influence was sufficient for King George III (who reigned between 1760-1820) to try out the theories at Weymouth – with a band on the beach playing God Save the King!

Later, his son Prince Regent (who reigned from 1820 to 1830 but was Regent from 1811), did likewise at Brighton.

The practice of taking a dip had thus achieved a double stamp of Royal approval.

The "seaside" was born.

Ever since, its reputation has been of a place for people to visit – for health, revitalisation and recreation.

Henceforth, it dawned on the inhabitants of previously insignificant coastal villages that a new potential beckoned – one that was later to become known as "tourism".

If transportation could be improved, the well-to-do could be encouraged to visit. There was a prospect of real economic benefit.

No longer would survival need to be skimped and scraped, through fishing or combing the beach for spoils of wreckage.

Initially, progress was inevitably slow.

New trends take time to become established – the further up the coast of England, the slower the momentum.

Here, the first recognition of the possible did not come much before 1770 – marked by the construction of the Skegness Inn, later to become the Vine Hotel, which survives to this day.

It was a start, but, even then, a further 100 years were to pass before the foot came down on the pedal.

What changed?

In Skegness, as in many towns and villages, the arrival of the railway was crucial.

Dating back to the 1770s, The Vine is the oldest hotel in Skegness and still as popular as ever.

It was in July, 1873, that the first train steamed in to what would have been the most basic of termini. But almost at a stroke, Skegness was opened up to a wider world.

Henceforth, anything was not only possible, it was probable!

No one will have felt the sense of opportunity more keenly than the area's largest landowner, the ninth Earl of Scarbrough.

There is no surviving record of who was aboard the first train to reach this hitherto remote point on the Lincolnshire Coast.

But among the band of pioneering rail passengers, the Earl was doubtless among the earliest.

Even before the arrival of the railway, Skegness' association with the Scarbrough family is longstanding.

To this day, it remains conspicuous – most notably in the name of the town's High School.

In the name Scarbrough, there is an 'o' missing after the 'b' – attributable to a registration error in the family deeds.

Given the circumstances, this is not inappropriate. There was never any meaningful connection with the town in Yorkshire of similar name – apart from a possibility that a forebear of the Earl may once have been a governor of the castle there.

The land in and around Skegness had passed from one noble landowner to another many times since the Middle Ages – almost like an extravagant ritual of pass-the-parcel.

But the name, Scarbrough, was chosen as if on a whim.

What an unfortunate irony! Its prevalence provides ongoing publicity for a seaside resort which just happens to be a main competitor to Skegness!

But back to the ninth Earl. His extraordinary influence has been comprehensively chronicled by eminent Skegness historian Winston Kime in a series of authoritive and brightly-written books which urgently deserve to be reprinted.

Suffice it to say that the Earl was born Richard George Lumley and inherited the title when his cousin died in 1856.

His decision, in about 1876, to create a new town was audacious – but it was partly a case of necessity being the mother of invention.

After a long spell of prosperity, agriculture had slumped – a situation that, alas, has been revisited at the start of the 21st Century.

Then, as now, there was a requirement to seek new ways of adding value to the land.

The Earl had a shrewd and inspired agent, Henry Tippet, and it was probably he who most emphasised the potential of converting what was no more than a humble fishing village to a new resort town by the sea.

Even so, it took incredible daring to embark on such an expensive venture.

It could all have gone horribly wrong, bringing financial ruin to the Earl and his family.

Instead, it was a brilliant success. A new resort town was created – one not just of pleasant tree-lined avenues but with its own seafront promenade.

The pleasure gardens – later to be renamed the Tower Gardens – were of particular distinction, created from a site used for storing coal that had been landed by ship locally from Tyneside.

Leases for the plots were sold off to various developers and architects, among them being T. C. Hine of Nottingham, establishing a link with the Robin Hood city that has thrived to this day.

But the Earl and his successors remained landowner and maintained a control which was as strict as that of any planning authority today.

What sort of man was the ninth Earl?

He was born in 1813 at Tickhill Castle, near Rotherham, but little is recorded about the character of an individual who laid the foundation for Skegness as it is today – his personality, his motivation, his tastes.

What makes his achievement all the more remarkable is that, soon after he succeeded to the earldom, a fall from his horse left him paralysed and without the use of either leg.

If it had not been for that fateful accident, would he still have channelled such energy into the creation of building a new town by the sea? Or would he have done other things?

No one will ever know. What is sure is that, for eight frenetic years – already in his 60s – he had the energy and stamina to oversee the start of an immense project, one which will never have been free from complication, frustration and expense.

Despite being disabled following a riding accident, the ninth Earl of Scarbrough retained the vision, energy and determination to create a new seaside resort (photo: courtesy, Earl of Scarbrough Estate.

The tragedy is that he may never have truly witnessed the first fruits of his initiative. In his later years, his eyesight rapidly failed.

By the time he died – on December 5, 1884 – he was almost totally blind.

Praise, too, for the enterprise, skill and energy of his staff and workmen.

Remember, in the days before mechanical diggers and sophisticated construction machinery, the labour all had to be performed by spades and shovels, horses and carts.

The glory of the newly-created town was its pier.

When it was opened in June, 1881, by the then Duke of Edinburgh, it measured 1,843ft, making it the fourth longest in Britain.

It had been constructed by contractors Head Wrightson and Co. of Hull – at a cost of £20,000.

There was initial criticism that the original Gothic archways of the pierhead were more in the style of a cemetery than a leisure attraction.

Although the entrance was subsequently to be revamped on several occasions, the complaints were overdone. There was nothing that could undermine its popularity during the next 97 years.

The wonder of piers is that they offer a trip to the sea with neither the peril nor the prospect of motion sickness.

That made the sixpence (2.5p) admission well worthwhile.

According to one statistic, the August Bank Holiday of 1882 brought no fewer than 20,000 visitors to the pier – many having arrived in Skegness by train for the sheer, unbelievable thrill of "walking the plank".

Not only that but, as time passed, it hosted a range of fabulous sideshows – from novelty stalls at the entrance to concerts and music hall entertainment at the end.

Alas, it was too good to last.

Like all seaside piers, the one at Skegness was, throughout its life, vulnerable to collisions – occasionally from whales but more likely from shipping.

On March 21, 1919, it was totally breached by one such vessel, the schooner Europa, in a needless accident attributed to the irresponsibility of its Dutch skipper.

But repaired, then reinstated, it survived . . . until the night of January 11, 1978.

When a violent storm blew up, nothing could prevent her from being shattered by the raging waves.

Remarkably, the 1000-seater theatre survived, and her contents were salvaged between tides until she, too, perished in October, 1985, after sparks from an unattended incinerator set alight the whole of the wooden structure.

Fortunately, many episodes in the life of the pier are recorded in old postcards, in a book by its late manager, Albert Thompson, and in a series of articles first published in the Skegness News by Edmena Simpson, then reprinted in a booklet by the same author.

Memories are wonderful, but to many – both residents and holiday-makers – there is no question the pier's demise has left a lingering, aching loss.

From time to time there has been speculation about rebuilding it in full, perhaps through funds from a wealthy benefactor or from the National Lottery, but that day has not come.

To their credit, the current owners, UK Piers, have made substantial investments, creating new or improved attractions in what little remains of the structure.

But to anyone who remembers the pier as it was, the soul has expired.

In its present form, it is but a reminder of Paradise lost.

Paddling on the beach – a popular therapy since the 1750s, and completely free.

During the period of its creation as a resort, Skegness must have been a vibrant community – full of the excitement of the new.

But apart from the pier, what man-made attractions were there to draw visitors from afar?

There sprang up a spiral amusement railway, and, on the beach, there was the wreck of an old ship, the Eliza, which served as a marine museum – but, in truth, not a great deal else.

As with the development of all towns, growth comes in fits and starts, it waxes and wanes.

By 1920, the exuberance of Skegness had begun to falter. The time had come for a new order.

To their undying credit, both vision and courage were demonstrated by the civic fathers of the day.

In January, 1922, Skegness Urban District Council made the bold decision to take out a mortgage enabling it to buy the foreshore from the Scarbrough estate.

The price paid – £15,750 – seems trivial now, but at the time it represented financial risk of a scale to generate misgivings aplenty.

But the initiative paid off – it sparked the next surge in the growth of the town.

Bracing sea air, wide open spaces, a chance to mingle (and exotic trees) – where better to be than Skegness?

An undoubted hero of this era was the council's engineer, surveyor and architect, Rowland Jenkins.

Nowadays, his immense contribution seems almost to have been forgotten. Mention of his name is seldom heard in civic circles.

Yet, during the almost monumentally long period he held sway – from 1912 to 1952 – he masterminded a second remarkable phase in the development of this famous seaside resort.

The new features were impressive – the Embassy ballroom, bowling greens, tennis courts, a bathing pool, a boating lake, the Suncastle solarium, a waterway, beachside walks, a ruined castle and an expanse of rose gardens.

It was Jenkins who transformed the foreshore into a huge pleasure park by the sea, sometimes incorporating ideas he brought back with him from walking tours in Italy and elsewhere on the Continent.

An example of the walk alongside the south boating lake – formerly known as the Axenstrasse – which, with its rustic fences, arches, bridges and castle ruin effect was designed to give at least a hint of the St. Gothard area of the Swiss Alps.

At the start of the 21st Century, despite decades of change, his vision persists. Almost all the amenities he created for the foreshore have survived.

Named after a famous Skegness actress, the Elizabeth Allan was one of the pleasure boats that used to make trips across The Wash until the rising level of the sandbanks became too serious an obstacle.

A testimony to Jenkins' vision and flair, coupled with a driving sense of purpose, is that so much was achieved during the 1930s – a decade when most of the world's economy was in deep depression.

Even as he developed the foreshore, Jenkins never lost sight of special importance in the overall scheme of the foreshore of the clock tower – its shape, its size and its historical significance.

When the pier was lost to the sea, the 56ft-high brick and stone tower assumed an even greater importance.

Built in 1899 by Edmund Winter of Liverpool to mark Queen Victoria's Diamond Jubilee, it remains the town's most notable landmark.

Looking down towards Lumley Road, Grand Parade, Tower Esplanade and South Parade, the grand old lady of Skegness – now slightly leaning – has seen and heard it all.

She has appeared on the front of millions of postcards, and she retains within her walls the secrets of generations of passers-by – residents and holidaymakers alike.

Some would say she is more demure than she is grand, and the noted architectural observer Nikolaus Pevsner described her flippantly as "Gothic, but not at all serious, with a Big Ben top".

That is as may be, but the clock tower is to Skegness what Nelson's column is to Trafalgar Square and what the Statue of Liberty is to New York – a symbol of pride and heritage.

What is more she, she is socially relevant – the traditional gathering point for the two highlights of the resort's social calendar.

Of these, one is the fancy dress celebration that marks the arrival of the New Year.

The other, in August, is the celebrity switch-on of the summer illuminations, usually by a figure from the world of showbiz whose presence is guaranteed to draw crowds of up to 10,000 holiday-makers and residents alike.

On August 8, 1977, that switch-on celebrity was Billy Butlin –

It was the last visit to the resort by a man who changed the character of British holidays.

The famous camp built in 1936 by Butlin just outside the town in Ingoldmells was not the first of its kind.

That accolade is sometimes said to belong to the one at Trusville, further up the coast towards Mablethorpe.

But, in fact, pleasure camps, if only of a rudimentary and ramshackle nature, are reckoned to date back to the 1880s.

Butlin's brilliance was in raising the concept to a new level of wondrousness.

Conscious of the vagaries of the British weather, his emphasis was on entertainment – both indoors and outdoors. He made life at his camps a perpetual celebration.

It was no drawback to Butlin that he was of limited education. Like all entrepreneurs, he was blessed with self-belief, enthusiasm, shrewdness, resilience, determination, knowledge of his chosen market and a willingness to take risks.

The more successful he became, the more these characteristics became self-reinforcing.

He epitomised the old saying that successful people make their own luck.

Born on September 29, 1899 in Capetown, South Africa, and subsequently brought up in Canada and Bristol, his childhood and teenage years were less than stable – firstly because of his parents' divorce and secondly because life with his mother was one of almost constant travel.

But, as he so emphatically went on to prove, insecurity can be a springboard for success.

Butlin's early career was spent operating hoopla stalls – firstly in Bristol with an uncle, then in Olympia, London, on his own account.

His curiosity and quest for fresh opportunities brought him to Skegness where, in 1925, his first venture was to set up a similar stall on a site off North Parade then known as The Jungle – close to where the County Hotel stands today.

In a happy-go-lucky holiday town, he immediately found himself at home – and he went from strength to strength.

He adapted his various ventures – including model cars, a slide, a haunted house and the first Dodgem bumper cars seen in Britain – to the tastes of visitors.

Holiday camp founder Billy Butlin – greatest leisure entrepreneur of the 20th Century (photo: courtesy, Butlins Archives).

But the project which opened one of the most famous chapters in the history of British holidays came at Easter, 1936, when Butlin established his first camp on 40 acres of what previously had been turnip fields.

What happened next is part of Britain's holiday lore: Hi-de-hi, wakey wakey, rise and shine, exercises before breakfast, Redcoats, knobbly knees contest, glamorous grandmothers and much else.

For 30 years, Butlin's was at the centre of the glorious heyday of British seaside holidays.

But, as always, the reminder returned – time changes everything. Butlin's was not invincible.

All businesses, however successful – particularly those focused on entertainment – run the risk of fatigue.

This was the fate of Butlin's in the 1960s – and it was further weakened by the threat from overseas.

The impact of cheap package holidays in the Spanish Costas offered the guarantee of unbroken sunshine, coupled with a flavour of the exotic.

In 1968, Butlin retired to Jersey, appointing his son, Bobby, as his successor.

Four years later, after two consecutive years of slumping profits, Butlin's was sold to the Rank Organisation for £44-million.

Thereafter, the business seemed to lose its way further, despite a major financial investment in 1986, coupled with a change of name to Funcoast World.

Butlin is reported to have once said that he wanted to be buried in Skegness. If so, it was a wish that went unfulfilled.

On retirement, he went to Jersey where he died and was buried in June, 1980.

In the year 2000, with the centre's name subsequently restored to Butlins (without the apostrophe) and in the wake of a further £50-million investment, the centre returned to private ownership with its acquisition from Rank by Bourne Leisure.

Since then the curve of its popularity seems to have returned to the upwards direction. Much of the old zest has been restored.

Whatever else, Butlins remains the best known brand in British holidays.

Even before Billy Butlin built his famous first holiday camp, Skegness' special reputation as a holiday resort was assured.

The achievements of men like the Earl of Scarbrough, Henry Tippet and Rowland Jenkins had, as it were, found an artistic expression.

Its appeal was captured in the Great Northern Railways poster depicting a portly fisherman skipping across the sands, with the slogan: Skegness is SO Bracing.

The Jolly Fisherman is the most famous imaginary figure in the history of the British seaside – commissioned by the railway in 1908 for a fee of nine guineas from the artist John Hassall.

The purpose was to promote cheap return excursions from London, Kings Cross to Skegness, the fare being three shillings (15p).

The picture underwent many adjustments – some of the earliest being performed by the artist himself.

Subsequent adaptations have often been far more radical and often controversial.

Silent salesman for Skegness – John Hassall's most famous creation, the Jolly Fisherman.

The Jolly Fisherman, in his various guises, has had scores of different applications – not just in Britain but all over the world.

At one moment, Jolly (as he is referred to locally) turns up in a promotional poster in the foyer of a hotel on the Spanish Costa del Sol, at the next he is adorning the walls of a massage parlour in Bangkok.

Why the enduring fascination? Who can say? Neither the picture nor the accompanying caption are of special intrinsic merit.

But though separately they may be of little creative impact, together they have struck a chord.

Strangely, for all the fame it brought him, a further 28 years elapsed before Hassall actually visited Skegness.

The Urban District Council presented him with a vellum certificate which afforded him the freedom of Skegness.

In a wry speech, Hassall acknowledged the honour – not least because it allowed him free use of deckchairs on the beach!

Hassall, who was originally from Deal in Kent, died in 1948, aged 79, at his home in Kensington Park Road, London – and in relative obscurity.

But his most famous creation, the Jolly Fisherman, lives on as a silent salesman for Skegness.

At the start of the 21st Century, how is the enduring popularity of Skegness to be defined?

Either by rail or road, the journey here is not quick or easy. Notwithstanding the example of the Norse invaders 1,100 years ago, the town can no longer be reached by sea.

Even with improvements since the opening of The Hildreds arcade in 1988, the shopping scene can hardly compare with those in the towns and cities from which Skegness draws most of its holiday visitors.

True, there are significant attractions such as Natureland, Panda's Palace, Church Farm Museum, the Embassy Centre and the Tower Gardens.

But hopes for a unique museum of the seaside or for some major all-weather hi-tec, interactive visitor attraction have yet to be fulfilled.

When, in the late-1990s, an ambitious scheme for a weather interpretive centre at a site on the foreshore was unveiled, it was turned down by planners.

Why then the lasting allure?

Is it the sight of the sea? No, it is not even visible from Grand Parade – the town's main promenade.

Is it the smell of the sea? No, with the prevailing winds blowing offshore, it is seldom detectable.

Then is it the cackling laughter of the herring gulls from their nests on the chimney rooves?

Again no. Unlike other seaside towns, no gulls breed in Skegness.

What then? Is it in its kiss? We're getting warm. It may be incapable of definition, but there is just 'something' about Skegness.

Perhaps it is the wide open spaces, the refreshing air, and the knowledge that, yes, the sea is just behind that big building on the right.

Or perhaps it is a feeling that it is good to be in such a friendly, welcoming resort – one with no unattractive pretensions to grandeur.

Whatever the reason – or combination of reasons – when the crowds gather at Bank Holidays or in the peak summer season, the sense of energy and vitality is palpable.

There's a party going on – not just for the young, but for people of all ages, including the elderly.

There's a huge beach and the sea, there are donkeys, ice creams, pubs, nightclubs, arcades, crazy golf, bowls, a funfair, foreshore foodstalls . . . and, yes, even a bit of a pier.

What is more, there is the chance to meet people, to relax to have lifted the humdrum of day-to-day life.

Even if only for a week, a weekend or just a few hours, that's livin'.

Everything combines to reinforce a sense of the exuberant, the carefree . . . and the reassuring.

Reassuring? Yes, look at that poster outside the Embassy! It's for a show by Ken Dodd.

Happiness! Didn't we see him at the pier theatre in the 60s – and he's still here 40 years later!

Skegness is a kaleidoscope . . . and a paradox. Like the waves out to sea, it is always the same, yet constantly changing.

For more than 120 years, the town has been a work in progress. It remains thus.

Long may Skegness – and the party – continue!